To Jeff, with best wishes of success and happiness,

Marinella Monk, MD

April, 2020

The cover is a background photograph of the Gulf of Mexico at Santa Rosa Beach, Florida, with smaller inset pictures of Dr. Marinella Monk

Marinella F. Monk, MD

You Are Not Alone

From Frog to Prince

YOU ARE NOT ALONE

By Marinella F. Monk, MD

Library of Congress Control Number
2009911195

This book is dedicated to the memory of my parents, Ioan and Marcella Mirea, to Beatrice, my beautiful daughter, and to my rock, my friend and my husband, Robert, with all my love, always.

Marinella F. Monk, MD

THE TWENTY THIRD PSALM

The Lord is my shepherd, I shall not want.
He maketh me to lie down in green pastures,
He leadeth me beside the still waters,
He restoreth my soul.
He leadeth me in the paths of righteousness
For his name's sake.
Yea, though I walk through the valley of
The shadow of death,
I will fear no evil, for thou art with me;
Thy rod and Thy staff they comfort me.
Thou preparest a table before me in the
Presence of mine enemies.
Thou annointest my head with oil;
My cup runneth over
Surely goodness and mercy shall follow
Me all the days of my life
And I will dwell in the house of the Lord
forever.

CHAPTERS

1.	Coping with hard times	1
2.	Face your reality	5
3.	Analyze your situation	7
4.	Develop a plan	9
5.	Act on your plan	11
6.	Get advice	13
7.	Your attitude	15
8.	When doubt lurks in the shadow	21
9.	Is your plan going to work?	25
10.	Will change be difficult?	29
11.	Perspective	33
12.	Overcoming limitations	35
13.	Unload, simplify, cleanse	41
14.	Visualize	45
15.	Learning	51
16.	Connecting	55
17.	Ban addiction	59
18.	Healing time	63
19.	Prayers for healing	67
20.	Appreciation	71
21.	Gratitude	73
22.	Your health	77
23.	Choose the right food	81
24.	What about alcohol?	87
25.	Exercise	89
26.	A promise	93

Marinella F. Monk, MD

27.	Anticipate the best	95
28.	Give your blessings	97
29.	Expand your horizons by travelling	99
30.	Learning from other cultures	107
31.	Home sweet home	111
32.	Conclusion	113
33.	Acknowledgements	115
34.	Reader reviews	119

In the middle of difficulties, lies opportunity."

Albert Einstein

Coping with hard times

This small book is intended to help us cope with the hard times we all face, one day or another. Although I hope that everyone is doing quite well, the reality is that a troubled economy, population explosion, and political tensions of global proportions have most of us struggling in these difficult times.

I do not offer a miraculous, instant solution to our daily problems. I don't believe there is such a thing, but if ever anyone does find a magic solution, I am most eager to hear it.

My message is a lot more humble; the reality is that we all deal with difficulties, and in many circumstances they seem insurmountable. We all think that this happens only to us.

We all need a little word of encouragement in times when we feel lost. And we all appreciate a little help in dealing with our problems, and I only hope to bring some clarity when you are standing in the middle of the storm, surrounded by thc fog of desperation.

Something you may not want to hear during a crisis, is that this may be, and probably is, your time and opportunity to change things for a better life.

I've seen it and heard it over and over again, from so many people, who say that change brought about by life's difficulties was the best thing that ever happened to them. So, if everything is perfect in your world, then congratulations and you have the envy of us all. If not, then take a moment to slow down and reconsider the direction your life is taking.

Now is the time to sort out what it is that you always wanted to do and did not have the time, the money, or the opportunity to achieve. If you look at your entire situation, you might see the stability and comfort that you desperately try to conserve, but circumstances have changed, and you may be about to lose everything you fought for.

Now is the time to consider if you are ready for big changes; now might be the time to dream big.

So, here we are, the time has come for this leap of faith, to fulfill that dream you never had the means, support, nor the courage to go for.

In my career as a medical doctor, I encountered many patients unable to continue their jobs because of injuries they had suffered. They were devastated, their entire universe collapsed and depression added to their other medical conditions. Not only were they in pain, and many times not able to sleep, but also in a short period of time they had to face financial, professional and familial difficulties.

I've seen my patients losing their self-esteem as providers, unable to assume their roles as heads of the family, or as father figures, feeling incapable and confused.

And here I was, making them angry telling that this could be the best thing that ever happened to them!

I was telling them all this because I could see their potential, and had a realistic expectation of what their physical abilities could be after recovery; I was pushing them because I saw them as whole human beings and I cared not only for their clinical improvement, but also for their feelings and their futures.

I have cried together with some patients when touched by their despair. But I have also cried with joy when the unthinkable occurred a year or so later, after they completely changed directions, and aimed for situations they never could dare to dream of before, and they were actually living those dreams.

Indeed, this was the best thing that could have happened to them!

Dear FRIEND, whoever YOU are, wherever YOU are, from now on, YOU are not alone. I am YOUR friend and I am here to help.

So, lets take a deep breath and get started!

Here is the reality, a mountain of tangled information, confusing and complicated. What to do?

Face your reality-Analyze-Organize-Plan-Act

Face your reality

It takes a great amount of courage to do what you just did. This is your first step, but it is a giant step.

You know that the problems are not going away if you ignore them, they will only accumulate, and complicate your life even more. No matter what, sooner or later they will catch up with you when you will be the least prepared.

So open the door, scream, and complain for as long and as much as you must to get it the tension out of your system. Then, gently close the door, shutting them out of your life.

Now sit down and make a list of those (darn) problems. Take all the time you need, and let the list be as long as necessary.

So what, we're facing the demon(s). Scary, isn't it?

Now, start another list and write down all the good things present in your life, all the blessings you can name; you will be surprised to see that this second list is a lot longer than the problem list. Feeling more reassured?

Analyze your situation

Now organize your problem list by categories and in the order of their urgency.

Identify the items to be resolved, clearly verify any potential mistake that you could eliminate swiftly and easily.

Under each problem listed, write your ideas about solving it, people to contact in regard to the problem or anyone that could help.

It is important to make sure that you did not forgot any hidden papers, documents or bills, out of your problem list; carefully review the figures and update them, one may cancel out others.

Then, gather the other members of your family, or persons directly involved with the reason of your trouble, and gently explain the situation, ask for their ideas, collaboration, and understanding.

Listen to any potential solution that one could bring to you that could make your task easier.

Develop a plan

We are never more vulnerable than when we lack directions, and don't deal with accumulating problems. Having a plan of action will help you to stay motivated, keep you grounded to reality, and prevent you from running from your problems again.

DON'T procrastinate any longer.

You must be realistic when structuring the basis of your plan, then start with priorities.

If it makes you feel more confident, begin with baby steps.

Establish a "war plan," clearly designate the person in charge of each project and the mode of action chosen for each area needing your attention. Make clear who is responsible and be specific as to what is everyone's designation, but reassure each member of the plan, that an open dialog is the rule, as is providing help and advice every time it is needed.

The secret here is not to try to solve problems the hard way, but the smart way.

Research all the areas where you have to intervene and contact others going through similar situations.

There is unlimited information available through the Internet where you can find help.

You could also find help from your professional, social, or religious circles. You will be surprised by the genuine concern, support, and generosity of people.

Keep accurate records and update them, particularly when you get new information while working on the elements included in these files.

You will benefit from creating a schedule of interventions. Make notes of all new information, contacts, recommendations, or plans of action of the file you are working on.

Act on your plan

Now that you have a plan, you will have the motivation to act. Moreover, you have a purpose.

Results will come only if you stay focused and apply strict discipline.

Remember this: motivation, focus, discipline.

No matter what, stay in the game and play it correctly.

Millions of people have great ideas all the time. Only the very few who stay focused and show good discipline ever realize these ideas.

This is the secret that makes the difference why some people never get anywhere, and others achieve great success.

Follow your schedule at the letter; do not get distracted by others.

No excuses!

Get advice

It would be wise to hear some other opinions about your situation and ways to solve the problems you are dealing with. You don't need to hear "I told you so." Get real help, from objective, well intended, and knowledgeable people.

Understand that ultimately YOU will make the final decisions, and knowing that, you will be more receptive to other ideas. It is good to expand your view of the situation requiring your attention, which will be very helpful when assessing your options. This will also give you a more accurate picture of the problem(s), as well as of the alternatives for solving them.

Nowadays, there is a wealth of information offered through media, internet, etc.; where one has access to research and to free legal counsel, and other valuable professional advice.

It will take a little more time, but good research will pay off substantially, if you make wiser choices.

Your attitude

It is important to take a look at your attitude during these hard times, and it could be a good thing to simply review your behavior.

One cannot always change or have control of the events in life; the only thing we can control is the way we react to them.

First to consider is how do we manage our temper. It is easy to panic, scream, and play the blame game. We all have our weaknesses and sensitive buttons, and we know what tender point will trigger the first blast. We all deal with this the best we can.

But a common denominator we humans have to struggle with is over reaction.

If there is one thing we need to learn in this lifetime, all of us, it is how to stop over reacting.

We do this, and we regret right after. We never solve a problem by over reacting, we only complicate our lives and disturb our relationships, and yet, we do it over and over again.

Instead, offer a simple act of kindness, unplanned and unselfish gesture toward your loved ones.

In this difficult time, you may argue that you have no money to spoil anyone. Well, money is not always necessary. Just do something sincere and nice. Pick a few wild flowers, write a little poem, or leave a little note close by with a few words from the heart.

Do a few things around the house that you don't have to, just because you are a sweetheart or a better person. You will create a little surprise, even a great shock, but what a great example!

Nowadays, we spend most of our time without family interaction. We work, we watch television, spend time on the computer, read, or play sports, but we forget about spending real quality time together. Think about gathering together and telling stories around a campfire just relaxing and having a good time.

Start a few new activities that include all family members, such as impersonations, imitations, clown contests, and you will have a few happy times together, that will cost you nothing, (well, maybe a little embarrassment!).

Dance, sing, and make the others follow; it is okay to make fool of yourself once in a while.

Laugh often; it is the best anti-stress therapy.

Remember that what is most important in your life is your family and the small group of your friends. You count on them for support and understanding, and in turn, they expect you to treat them well.

They are the last ones we should abuse in their patience and love, although we often do so, since they may be the only ones to tolerate it. And don't forget to thank them and show them your appreciation as the recovery process goes on.

The world is in big need of goodness, and the smallest act of kindness could make a big difference.

We don't have to go far to bring assistance to others, and if everyone would behave the way they would like others to behave, our world would be closer to heaven.

Remember Jean Valjean from "The Miserables" by Victor Hugo? Jean Valjean suffered from unspeakable injustice and spent more than 20 years in a jail working hard and inhuman labor. All this was because he stole a loaf of bread to feed his starving nephews and nieces.

Finally freed, he wandered the French countryside as a broken man, his heart full of resentment for the whole world.

By now, the only way he knew how to behave was to rob, hate, and defend himself like a cornered animal.

But everything changed when a priest offered him shelter one night. Jean Valjean robbed him, taking valuable silver objects, but the priest defended him when he was apprehended by policemen, and told them that it was a gift to Jean Valjean. With this simple but so generous gesture, his whole life changed forever, and from a miserable thief, Jean Valjean became an exceptional man, his life dedicated to good and noble causes.

All this happened because of the act of incredible generosity by a man, who understood that treating another human being kindly, could awaken the sacred part inside him. We all can change for the best, and this may be all that is required for someone to change an entire life.

If you look around you will see so many people who, alone or creating various organizations, bring hope and support to others.

You, too, can find a way to touch someone's soul and make a difference in this world.

When doubt lurks in the shadows

You will wonder if you can go on, question your aptitude, and have a low opinion of yourself.

You are frightened and depressed, which makes a change in direction or attitude even harder.

But Dear Friend, remember this: everyone, every single creature has been given amazing gifts.

I never encountered someone who did not have a special aptitude or talent, or who was not graced by some beautiful feature.

Just look around, every day we see in the news, places where we go, examples of exceptional people who overcome the most impossible odds, and who have offered their contribution in making this world a better place.

A little boy, afflicted with muscular dystrophy, before dying at a very tender age, spread beauty and gave hope through his poems.

A little girl did the same, and I am sure there

are many more, who could have very rightly so, wrapped themselves in their suffering. They had all the excuses in the world to feel sorrow for themselves, angry that destiny gave them a short life to live.

Instead, they found peace and gave us hope that there is always something worth living for, no matter how long or short is the time we have ahead of us.

What is important is how we live our lives, how we mark our passage on this place called Earth, and if we knew how to share our happiness with others.

Ludwig van Beethoven, (1770-1827), attended school only until the age of 10. His father, a talented tenor, but also an alcoholic, saw his great musical inclination and initiated the young Ludwig in playing the piano, violin and organ.

Beethoven's father, aware of his son's unique talents, started "exhibiting" him at age of five. The young Ludwig began supporting his family at an early age, since his father was not capable of doing so. He became head of the family after his mother died, taking care of his two brothers while he was still in his teens.

Beethoven was self-educated, teaching himself from classics, Homer, Plato, and Plutarch, but also he studied contemporary art and literature.

At the age of 17, when living in Vienna, and aware of missing years in his education, he went to the University and studied philosophy and German literature.

The genius of Beethoven was quickly recognized and admired by other composers, such as Mozart, Bach, Haydn, Salieri, and others.

Beethoven was afflicted early in life by losing his hearing; over the years he became more isolated into his own world, hearing his music in his mind only.

Toward the end of his life when conducting the premiere of his famous 9th Symphony, he had to be turned around by the concertmaster, to see the audience delirious of admiration.

Beethoven could not hear his own music, yet he transcended his own misery and left behind incredible beauty.

Beethoven 's life inspired Romain Rolland, winner of the 1915 Nobel Prize in literature, to write “L’Ame Enchantee” (Enchanted Soul), a novel that touched many in their search for real values and character.

Is you plan going to work?

You will wonder if the transformation of your self and your life is going to succeed. Will I make it? Will this work for me?

All theses questions are legitimate; they actually should occur in any journey, in order to assess if we are on the right track, if there is any need for adjustments.

While keeping the vision of the general picture in focus, we need a lot of flexibility and clarity of judgment to avoid bad decisions.

So, the answer is YES, you are going to succeed! Why? Because you are supposed to! In a life time one will change careers, will "recycle" at least two to three times. When we are young, many times we take a job by necessity and later we look into something more fulfilling. Later on, we might have to readjust because of a lost job, retirement, or new orientations.

We are "wired" to change. Our body and mind offer amazing mechanisms to improve and adapt to new situations.

Our body has the ability to heal most damages inflicted on it. Just think about watching the daily progress of a skin laceration in its natural self-repair process.

More and more we learn about the great potential of stem cell use in healing devastating diseases. I am very excited about the scientific progress that soon will allow our own adult stem cells to restore our health.

The perfection of our creation is of an almost mystical beauty: we have inside us everything we need to heal. We only need to find it and use it.

New scientific discoveries have shown that our body, this totally autonomous marvel, which does not need to be plugged in, nor charged with batteries, is able to radiate more heat per cubic centimeter than the sun.

Our organism is more efficient than the center of our solar system!

So how can we doubt any longer the awesome capabilities of our bodies to repair our lives?

And then, I believe that there is a lot more

coming to our assistance than we can even comprehend.

Astrophysicists are now researching into the black matter and the black energy that makes up 75% of our universe and is still totally mysterious to us. They are also studying the presence of multiple dimensions.

Nevertheless, the astrophysicists acknowledge that since the cradle of history, some people believed that something more than our physical existence must be present.

So, here we are, the physics and the metaphysics are coming together, in order to confirm the complexity of our own universe.

The spirituality entering our lives, whether or not we accept it or even admit it, is a fundamental element that could empower all our actions.

It is my profound belief that spirituality completes our lives, giving sense, balance, and strength to our existence.

Will change be difficult?

It will probably be both difficult and easy. Making small and big changes will depend not only on the circumstances, but also on our state of mind.

One of the most difficult things we adjust to is change; we just don't like change! Somewhere inside us, we feel more secure with our habits; we don't like leaving our comfort zone.

Here is one example; the distance between the railway tracks has always been, exactly 143.5 centimeters, or 4 feet 8 1/2 inches. And, why is it such an odd number, instead of a round number?

When the first train carriages were built, starting around 1830, railroad workers used the same gauge for building the horse-pulled carriages, which were already used for wooden rail back in 1550's in the mines in Europe.

Those gauges were measured based on the distance between the wheels of the carriages, which themselves, were based on the width of the old roads used in those times.

Why were the roads built to that width? To have the answer we have to go back into the distant history of the Romans. The Romans built a great network of roads, used by two horse chariots, and they considered that the best distance for two horses side by side to run, was 143.5 centimeters.

So, we kept the same measurements for our modern high-speed trains.

Furthermore, this habit continued when we built the space shuttle; although the space engineers decided that the fuel tanks should be wider, they were manufactured in Utah, and therefore, needed transportation via train to the Space Center in Florida.

By now, you guessed, the tunnels through which the trains transporting the tanks had to go, could not accommodate anything that wide. So even the space engineers had to accept the Roman's measurements!

It seems that on certain occasions our habits become traditions, and they have their reason and place in our lives.

But insisting on keeping bad situations will

only maintain this false impression of security, for we already know that continuation of the same life style has failed us.

When your mind is set and you decide clearly where you want to go, then you will feel "supercharged" and you will accomplish things that a very short while before you considered impossible.

Of course, it would be ideal to have help from all directions, but honestly you cannot expect that.

In my own experience, after completing my medical studies at one of the Universities of Medicine in Paris and acquiring all my diplomas and specialty, I wrote my thesis and started my own medical practice.

Then, a few years later, here I was again, coming to the US, going through the process of rebuilding my medical career. I went through the agony of getting my medical equivalences, internship, and residency in a new specialty.

For years it was a struggle, with three teenagers at home, exhausted from being on call and caring for my family,.. and broke.

It would have been a lot easier if I had the diplomas handed to me on a silver plate, but it did not come in that way, nor in a lottery ticket. I had to work hard for many years, overcome doubts, but what satisfaction at the end!

I would not have it any other way. And consider this: when I came to United States, I did not speak any English!

Everything comes with its price in efforts and dedication, but every achievement brings you satisfaction, knowledge and makes you grow. It is such a fulfilling experience.

A proper state of mind is essential in everything you do in life, particularly when making major changes.

Keeping clear in mind what you want to achieve and why, will keep you energized and help you through difficult moments.

Perspective

There is the story of the three masons who were asked about their profession.

The first answered, “I lay bricks one on the top of the other, all day long." The second said, “I work hard to feed my family." Finally, the third mason answered proudly, “I build cathedrals."

The three masons were doing the same work, but each of them valued their craft differently, and as a consequence, experienced a different drive and satisfaction from their profession.

Overcoming limitations

History or daily News tell us about so many people afflicted with either physical or "mental" limitations, accomplishing the impossible, and leaving exceptional examples in their paths.

These people teach us that there shouldn't be anything stopping us from achieving our goals. Their experience tells us that there are unexpected capacities and unique gifts in all of us.

Stephen Hawking, world-renowned theoretical physicist whose career spans over 40 years, brought his contribution to the fields of cosmology and quantum gravity.

Hawking is afflicted by a form of amyotrophic lateral sclerosis, and the disease has progressed over the years leaving him almost completely paralyzed.

He is able to communicate only through a computerized voice synthesizer especially designed for him; nevertheless, his exceptional mind is untouched, and the disease did not prevent him from graduating from Cambridge and Oxford with high honors.

Despite the fact that his physical condition worsened, Hawking was elected one of the youngest Fellows of the Royal Society in 1974, became Commander of the Order of the British Empire in 1982, and Companion of Honor in 1989.

Mr. Hawking has just been awarded the Rivera Medal of Freedom.

I had the privilege to attend one of his conferences years ago, and I continue to follow his work through his scientific programs. This is the way I learned that he was the first quadriplegic to float in zero gravity when flew in a comet of the Zero Gravity Corporation and could move freely the first time in 40 years!

Stephen Hawking describes himself as lucky despite his disease. Because of its slow progression, Hawking could make influential discoveries and has “a very attractive Family," as he describes it in his own words.

Personally I was fortunate to be in contact with incredible people that inspired me and served as models of determination and courage.

One of them is Doctor Agnes Moon, my mentor and Director of the Rehabilitation Training program, during my postgraduate resident attendance in the Physical Medicine and Rehabilitation program at EVMS in Norfolk, Virginia.

Although wheelchair bound from a car accident that happened while coming home after a long night call, Doctor Moon finished her training and specialized in Physical Medicine and Rehabilitation.

Her energy, knowledge, and humor were sources of daily motivation for all of us, the tired and penniless residents. She was hard on herself, but she would also scold non-compliant patients: for she was in the same situation as theirs, and found no excuses for them to give up hope.

Doctor Moon will always have a special place in my heart for her encouragements, kindness and great passion for life; for the great example she represented to us, not retreating into a world of sorrow, but bringing her contribution, helping and inspiring others afflicted with physical disabilities.

Georg Friedrich Haendel (1685-1759), the great composer of the famous "Water Music" and numerous other beautiful musical works, had difficulties with his eyesight. Toward the end of his life he became totally blind, but he continued his career until he died.

Despite of his loss, Haendel left behind vast and splendid musical masterpieces.

Wolfgang Amadeus Mozart (1756-1791), genius musician, although he lived only 35 years, left an extraordinary mark in this world with his art. Although during his life, Mozart new some moments of recognition and success, he died poor and was buried in a common grave.

There is a legend telling that, when the young Mozart was only about 5 years old, his father, Leopold, took him to be introduced to the Bishop of Passau. There, the little Wolfgang was waiting in a frigid anti-chamber for hours. After a while, his small hands and fingers became numb, the child went to the harpsichord, climbed on the chair, his feet not touching the floor, and started playing.

It is said that it was there when he composed

his famous Minuet K2, and since then Mozart's music was described as "a smile through tears" for his entire life.

Randy Pausch, professor of computer science at Carnegie Mellon University, refused to give up during his fight with pancreatic cancer, and continued his lectures inspiring millions.

He talked about fulfilling one of his childhood dreams. Pausch lost his battle with cancer in July 2008, but he celebrated life and decided to have fun until the end. Pausch created an animation based teaching program for high schools and college students and co-founded Carnegie Mellon Entertainment Center, for artists and engineers.

In The Last Lecture, Pausch stated that the lecture was for his three children. He was aware of his impending death, but he wanted to reach his children through his writings, even after his disappearance.

I know that we could go on forever with examples, so many were the ones achieving the "impossible", no matter the length of their time on Earth.

Unload, simplify, cleanse

In order to help the process of change, and considering new orientations in our lives, it would be very timely to sort out relations, social activities, and even home surroundings that might clutter our space and mind.

While we are reviewing our lives, we are seeing ourselves from a different angle if we want to honestly analyze what we should change. This is the perfect time to reconsider from a new perspective what or who is really a positive presence for us.

Somewhere deep inside us we know what troubles us, what feels heavy or inappropriate. Having to make changes, is an excellent occasion to discard unnecessary objects, as well as activities; it is a good excuse to get rid of toxic relationships poisoning our lives, which keep us "stuck" in a bad situation.

YOU made a great decision in your life, you took your future in your own hands, and that empowers you. While you are feeling strong about making changes and transforming your life for the best, why not cleanse your surroundings and your soul from whatever clouds your vision and drags you down.

Simplify your life, cleanse and unload, and you will feel so much lighter, you will feel liberated!

One of the most sensitive subjects is how to handle difficult relatives. What you should know for sure is that they are in ALL families. We can choose our profession, spouse, lover, even our shirt in the morning, but not our family. What we can choose though, is with whom and what kind of relationship we are willing to maintain. This is true with friends, coworkers, or other acquaintances.

What I am trying to convey, is that it is good to offer help and assistance to ones in need. You may be a great source of advice as well. But you have to learn when it is time to stop, as you will do with your own children, in order to let them learn how to fly on their own.

Excesses between 'givers' and 'takers' are a threat to stability in all relationships. We must protect ourselves, our families, and our friends against creating these imbalances.

We must not over-burden others, nor can we

permit others to over-burden us unfairly. If we allow these cycles to form, they will create real havoc in relationships when they will ultimately be interrupted.

Some of the relatives you are probably helping for years, knowing perfectly well that they are taking advantage of you, playing your emotions or, worse, your feelings of guilt, will not make the effort to change as long as they are assisted by you. I am saying assisted because, unintentionally, you enable them in their habits.

You must know, and this may help you in your decision of letting go, that as long as they don't move on with their own lives, they cannot fulfill their destinies.

I am not saying that you have to discontinue completely your relationships with them, or to argue with them; very gently tell them that you do this out of love, and you are always available for advice and the appropriate help.

You are given a genetic makeup from your parents, you have been raised in a particular cultural background, over which you have no choice; you can choose, however, who you become while fulfilling Your Own destiny.

Also get rid of all negativity lurking from the dark corners of your consciousness or your surroundings.

Negative thoughts are destructive; they cloud our reason and set our minds going in wrong directions.

It is normal to have doubts, to question from time to time if we are on the right track. This will also allow us to reconsider our decisions, make corrections when needed, and the results are positive.

But negativity attracts more negative actions, events, and people. It is like opening the lid to a dark well, looking down, and falling into it.

You have already made the right decision by choosing a better life for you and your loved ones.

Let this positive change be the moment when you decided to open the door to the light. Think of stepping into a new world you want to experience, a world of goodness, joy and beauty.

Visualize

Part of making a plan is to envision with clarity your final goal. Visualization is one of the "techniques" that have been applied by many in order to obtain surprising results.

Practically all of us have drawn or painted at some point in life; we chose the subject, colors, and shapes. We start with a blank piece of paper or canvas, and from there we create the image we have in mind.

Architects first design the structure and appearance of a house, building, or monument; then little by little, we see coming off the ground what first was only in their imagination.

In the same way, you have to paint your life; bring in your favorite subjects, create your own dreams, and put them inside the frame of your life.

Visualization will also allow you to find quiet moments of reflection, meditation, and dialog with yourself.

Mostly, you will find the moments for

PRAYER. Praying could bring you peace and comfort, but also strength and reassurance.

Many reputable medical studies prove the mysterious but real power of prayer.

During those double blind studies, patients admitted in the acute cardiac care units at different hospitals across the country, were randomly designated to groups of volunteers who prayed for their quick recovery.

Other patients in the study were not chosen by the computer to be part of the prayer group. Patients, physicians and medical staff, families, etc., did not know to what group the patient belonged.

The results were astonishing, showing clearly, in all studies and with significant probability value, that the patients who were prayed for, had a greater rate and speed of recovery.

And it is important to mention that the praying volunteers had no names, nor location of the person they were praying for, who in many circumstances were located thousands of miles away.

Visualization is also utilized by patients suffering from cancer and other severe medical conditions, and appeared very useful as an additional method in the treatment, or other coping and support mechanisms.

Through meditation, you will discover powers unknown to you and you might find a wealth of resources you could use, talents you could discover that will surprise you.

Learning to know yourself will help you make things easier in life, and will help you grow as a person.

When I was telling you to get help, I was also referring to the infinite energy and power of the Universe.

Some people will call it the Light, God, Universal Mind, Grand Creator, etc. No matter the name you give or pray to, men have known from the beginning of time that there are greater forces than ourselves.

Alfred Einstein, the physicist who invented the theory of relativity, said also, and I'm paraphrasing him, that the more he knows about science, the closer he gets to God.

He also said that God does not play dice with the Universe, but everything is interconnected and has a meaning.

Quantum physicists believe that the entire Universe emerged from thought.

It is perhaps good to consider that when you visualize something you actually help to materialize that idea, consciously or unconsciously, and bring it into your reality.

During this journey, look for signs that might tell you if you are on the right path. When something does not look or happen the way you would expect, it might be a sign that you need to reconsider your direction, for there are no accidents.

The Divine comes to your aid, preventing you from making mistakes, and if you pay attention, and give respect to these signs, you may see where they lead you or try to tell you.

When a Government nomination is made, and the elected person is sworn in, traditionally during the ceremony that person will wish for "divine guidance" while performing their public service, including the Justices of the

Supreme Court, who are usually elected for their life time.

James Redfield in his “Celestine Prophecy” talks about coincidences; you might have heard about in his writings relating to the emerging Spiritual Renaissance on Earth in the 1990’s. Some consider his books controversial, although many supported the idea of an era of spiritual awakening, which was quite new at the time. Redfield considered that coincidences are the signs one should look for, as guidance through their journey.

You heard in many instances that staying positive is important. Being positive refers to all actions of your life, in particular, your words.

Making constant negative affirmations concerning your acts and projects means that you don't actually believe in them. Your negative words, including your thoughts, automatically cancel out the good message you want to send into the Universe.

The words will become reality, and the reality is the one you first express in words, spoken or unspoken. This is why it is so important for you to affirm with conviction what you want.

The Bible is still a great source of confirmation that acknowledging your thoughts, feelings and intentions through words, will eventually manifest as reality.

You might remember what Jesus said: “If ye abide in me, ye shall ask what ye will, and it shall be done unto you.” (John 15:7)

Another citation said, ”A good man out of the good treasure of his heart bringeth forth that which is good; and an evil man out of the evil treasure of his heart bringeth forth that which is evil: for of the abundance of the heart his mouth speaketh.” (Luke 6:45)

“Pleasant words are as an honeycomb, sweet to the soul, and health to the bones.” (Proverbs 16:23)

I agree that making these affirmations is a matter of faith. But regardless of whether one is a believer or not, in order to achieve anything in life, it takes a certain amount of faith.

Learning

In our modern society, we tend to judge everything by its appearance; our actions are directed by the concrete perception of the reality. We are analytical, practical, and we consult and compare all data we can get our hands on. And all this is good and rational. Not only should we continue using our intellect, but also we need to continue to grow in knowledge and experience.

We hear all the time that knowledge opens all doors in life, and this is true. Knowledge gives to us a larger understanding of our lives and the Universe; knowledge gives us the thrill of comprehending how things work, and makes us feel confident.

During the changes and growing pains, we also learn a great deal about many subjects and ourselves.

You will be very surprised to discover how different you will feel when you start analyzing your actions and your character. You will perhaps find out that others see you very differently than you would think. All this is normal; it is part of evolving, growing wiser.

Paulo Coelho, an existentialist, is the writer of 'The Alchemist' and 'The Zaire'. These books have been a wonderful source of inspiration to me. Mr. Coelho tells an interesting story about our own image: two firefighters come out from a house where they just put out the fire; one has his face black with soot, the other's is still clean. Which one do you think will wash his face?

It will actually be the one with clean face: he looks at his comrade, sees his dirty face and thinks his must be dirty as well, and goes to clean up. The firefighter who has his face covered with soot, looking at the other and seeing his clean face, assumes that his is fine, and does not need to wash.

This metaphor is for us to understand about our own perception of how we look or behave.

The same paradox has been observed on many other occasions, and in certain instances, governs our relationships, making us draw the wrong conclusions about the way others see us.

This is why it is so important to learn about ourselves and pay REAL attention to the others, so we don't persist in the same false assumptions. We could avoid so many misunderstandings and improve our relationships if we correctly interpreted the feedback from others.

Learning and acquiring knowledge could be in many instances the key that opens new doors for you.

Connecting

We talked about connecting with our inner selves and each other; we established how important is the quality of our relationships, in our search for happiness.

Connecting with higher powers is a way of using ALL the sources that are at our disposal, and everyone should consider higher interventions in the major steps we take in our lives.

Our minds and souls should draw even more knowledge and strength from the Universal Knowledge and Energy, presented as gifts to us.

Only when body and mind work in harmony, does a person become whole.

Connecting is also creating our own Circle of Love. While projecting a different image of our selves, it is important to consider what kind of feelings we send out.

Kindness, respect, generosity, and goodness are all acts of love. Initiating those actions will start your Circle of Love. You are sending a clear message to the Universe, and like a boomerang, your actions will come back to you.

This is a very real phenomenon, well described by many authors.

I will, however, recommend you to read "The Secret," by Rhonda Byrne; this book could be a transforming experience. Byrne brings up quite strong arguments about manifestation of what one has in his mind.

She bases her writings on extensive referral to well known people, from ancient to present times. It could give you hope and confirmation of what you might already know.

The Circle of Love could become a great source of happiness to you, and you will learn how to heal through love. Sometimes, in order to move on and find your peace, you might have to forgive.

Forgiveness, the supreme act of love, is one of the most difficult to accept, but how liberating, how purifying to the soul this could be.

A Persian proverb says: "Love is a disease no

one wants to get rid of. Those who catch it never try to get better, and those who suffer do not wish to be cured."

Another marvelous example of transforming bad events into a good outcome, can be found in the book "The Shack," by William Paul Young. It is the story of a family going through the agony of the worst tragedy that could afflict any parents.

Just as in the story unfolding in the book, you could find the support you look for. The characters question the reasons for the story's dramatic events, and, in the end, find God and their peace.

And just as the family is crushed by a terrible sorrow, blinding their ability to comprehend the events, you might have similar feelings of loss and anger. God comes to guide them through these trying times, appearing as a large black woman who likes to cook and who laughs a lot; a She God, who does not judge but offers unconditional love.

Unexpected, but also so much more human and so much closer to our terrestrial life.

Ban addiction

During my medical practice, I started noticing the devastating effects of addiction; we all are aware of this social phenomenon, but when witnessing some of my own patients' behavior, and having to deal with them at the individual level, this issue becomes so much more real.

Interestingly enough, all addicts will have a few common ways of dealing with others: above all, they do not consider themselves addicted, they will deny even in the most evident situations, and when confronted with hard facts, will come up with the most ridiculous stories.

Another common fact is that they think this is not a problem in their lives, that they can handle it and quit anytime they want, and are totally oblivious to the dangers to which they subject themselves and others.

Only after a dramatic event, will they admit their problem and consider detoxification to avoid legal sanctions.

Relapses are frequently seen.

For a long period of time considered a taboo subject, now addiction is discussed openly, and with the help of the media, the general population is informed, unfortunately too often, about tragic accidents, consequences of people acting under the influence of drugs or alcohol.

Doing drugs is not only bad for the users and the ones they could be in contact with, but also for introducing and maintaining dealers and other shady characters with unhealthy ways of living, and who, sooner than later, will get in trouble with the law.

These individuals could bring you more complications and they are only after your money, the money you are already having difficulty to earn.
They are NOT your friends!

There is not, in my opinion, anything more heart breaking to witness, than the newborn of an addicted mother; the poor baby comes into this world in full withdrawal, and its chances of having good health and a caring family are limited.

In my practice, I do not do drug Rehabilitation,

but I help my patients to monitor their medications and take the strict minimum for very specific conditions, and only if no other type of treatment is sufficient or available.

Often, life style changes help not only personal problem solving, but heal us as well.

I feel personally hurt when I see people taking advantage of my compassion and trust, and every time I have dismissed a patient, it has been a big disappointment to me.

As we consider changing our ways, cleansing our body and mind, and getting rid of any actions that could take hold of our will, are essential as well.

Drugs, smoking, or drinking excessively are serious addictions, but gambling and anger fits should also be considered bad enough habits, that one should seek a radical change.

Taking complete control over our actions, thoughts and body is fundamental to any positive change.

A good life could not even be considered if we don't give up addiction.

Healing time

While reorganizing our lives, we are putting order and harmony in our existence.

This is similar to a healing process. During these fundamental changes, we are healing our life, and we also learn that we have the ability, along with the scientific knowledge and intervention, to bring in the use of the higher powers in helping healing our mind and body.

Lately, under stress and various worries, you may have felt like a bruised soul, licking your wounds in a corner, and wondering what would be next.

But slowly, making progress on your way of great transformations, you will experience more and more that you are emerging stronger, more confidant and more in control of your situation.

You analyzed your problems, and started by solving or discarding some of them. The veil of doubt is lifting; the fog of confusion is less dense. Now, feeling better, please allow yourself this healing time that your body and soul is craving.

Getting in touch with your inner self will help you to know more about who you are, and about the problems you still struggle with.

It is time to slow down, take some quiet moments, and be gentle with yourself. You deserve a little pat on the shoulder, and compensation for your efforts.

Hope, through hard work, along with Faith, will work as a cure of your whole being, spiritual as well as physical.

Divine healing is possible through God's word. Psalm 107:20, "God sent His word and Healed."

Remember again the power of the word.

"Son, attend to my words; incline thine ear unto my sayings. For they are life unto those that find them, and health to all their flesh." (Proverbs 4:2022)

Indeed, God's word will heal your body, for God's word is medicine that works through spiritual ways.

I would advise you to seek help from your

doctors. I have the strong belief that God inspires every doctor, scientist, researcher, and for that matter every person asking his help, so his work could be done in an infinity of His divine interventions.

I personally pray prior to treating my patients, and give thanks for guidance and aid God gives me to heal, through my mind and my hands.
It is why I encourage you to enhance the chances of your healing through prayer.

We already discussed the power of prayer in order to achieve your goals; now it is time to appreciate prayer as a powerful way to obtain the best results during the healing process.

Of course, all depends on your faith, for if you don't have faith, this won't apply to you.

I respect anyone's beliefs, and I will not feel offended if this chapter would not go along with your own vision of things.

But if you want to pray, here are a few examples that might help you and you may include them in your time of meditation.

Prayers for healing

"Jesus is the Lord of my life. Sickness and disease have no power over me. I am forgiven and free from sin and guilt." (Cor. 1:21,22)

"Jesus bore my sickness and carried my pain. Therefore I give no place to sickness or pain."

"For God sent His Word and healed me." (Psalm 107:20)

"I am alive unto God and by his stripes I am healed and made whole." (Rom. 6:11; 2 Cor. 5:21)

"You have given me abundant life. I receive that life through Your Word and it flows to every organ of my body bringing healing and health." (John 10:10; 6: 63)

"No evil will befall me, neither shall any plague come near my dwelling. For You have given Your Angels charge over me. They keep me in all my ways. In my pathway is life, healing and health." (Psalm 92:10, 11; Prov. 12:28)

"I present my body to God for it is the temple

of the living God. God dwells in me and His life permeates my spirit, soul and body so that I am filled with the fullness of God daily." (Rom. 12:1,2; John 14:20)

"Heavenly Father, through Your Word You have imparted Your life to me. That life restores my body with every breath I breathe and every word I speak." (John 6:63; Mark 11:23)

"Every organ and tissue of my body functions in the perfection that God created it to function. I forbid any malfunction in my body in Jesus' name." (Gen. 1:28,31)

"Father, Your Word has become a part of me. It is flowing in my bloodstream. It flows to every cell of my body, restoring and transforming my body. Your Word has become flesh; for You sent Your Word and healed me." (James 1:21; Psalm 107:20; Prov. 13:3)

"The law of the Spirit of Life in Christ Jesus has made me free from the law of sin and death; therefore, I will not allow sin, sickness or death to lord it over me." (Rom. 8:2; 6:13,14)

"The same Spirit that raised Jesus from the dead dwells over me, permeating His life through my veins, sending healing throughout my body." (Rom. 8:11)

"Lord, You have blessed my food and water and have taken sickness away from me. Therefore, I will fulfill the number of my days in health." (Ex. 23:25,25)

If you find inspiration from these few lines, read Charles Capps' "God's Creative Power for Healing," or you could make your own declarations. Your body will respond to the demands of your spirit.

If you belong to a different religious upbringing, or if you are a free thinker, there is an immensely rich choice of readings that could inspire you, within your believes and faith.

I particularly enjoy reading from time to time, 'The 72 Names of God', a meditation book of Kabbalah.

Each page is a prayer to one of the 72 Hebraic names of God, providing specific help in the areas of your life when you may need intervention.

It is believed that Kabbalah's origins go back to the 10th century BC, and is described as the main Jewish esoteric doctrine; although considered necessary in the study of Torah, some Jews reject it as heretic to traditional Judaism. This could be because its teachings show the relationship between the infinite and eternal Creator, and the finite and mortal universe of His creation.

When you read this book, the big surprise is that it really belongs to all men of all times, for it refers to the universe and human nature, the purpose of existence, and how to attain spiritual realization.

I would recommend you to read ‘The 72 Names of God’. It is simple, brings the Light into finding spiritual energy, and it is quite beautiful.

Just read the meditation number 63 name of God “Appreciation."

Appreciation

"I am quiet, and my soul opens.

As I think about my life, I see all that is good.

All that I sometimes fail to see is because of my own darkness.

I am filled with gratitude.

The light of the Creator shines upon me, and I am filled with abundance and joy.

As I take time each day to appreciate all of my blessings, the Light fulfills my desire.

I live fully in each moment.

Instead of looking back with regret, I concentrate on appreciating what I have now, and what I will continue to have."

Gratitude

It is in the human nature to complain; for some reason we feel better getting things off of our chest. It is like throwing worries far away from us, just by the sheer rejection of them.

Deep inside us, however, we know that bad things happen to all of us, we have dealt with difficult issues, and things could actually be a lot worse.

When events are not the most favorable, is the best time to look at the good aspects of our lives, and count our blessings.

Being grateful is a state of awareness of the good things present in our life. In a previous chapter I recommended making a list of the negative and positive things you could name. It is a good start just to review a situation that you might consider a lot worse than it really is.

Be honest and add all the valuable elements you see about yourself, as well as your family, career, place of living, or the support system you might have.

Learning how to see beauty around us, giving

thanks for a sunny bright day or the rain we need, blooming trees and flower fields, birds' concerts and glorious sunsets, even on our way rushing to work, could slow us down and fill our spirit with joy.

Showing gratitude means also giving appreciation to people when they help, encourage us, or simply they are kind to us. Every time someone is there for you, respond in an appreciative manner; show that you don't take anything for granted.

All this is so obvious, and again, in the middle of our troubles, we often forget to respond to many acts of unsolicited and gentle attention.

Then, consider your past and try to remember the unexpected events that occurred at the time you were the most in need of a celestial intervention.

One would be surprised to see how many of the people around us give the testimony of their own experience, when we bring up the subject of the miracles we lived.

When you are particularly down, you might find comfort in reading other people's touching and inspiring stories.

"Angels on Earth" is a publication one could appreciate in difficult times, as well as at any other moments, by reading about someone else getting help through miraculous interventions.

There are so many touching stories that would bring tears into anyone's eyes. (I even caught my husband tearing up a few times!).

I agree that no one could at the present times explain these interventions; perhaps because we are not evolved enough, because we have a lot more to learn and discover, and because our comprehension is still limited.

But more and more, we have to admit the presence of powers, however mysterious and above our explanation, yet so real and so divine in their nature.

We might benefit from just accepting certain events, even if we cannot control or explain them.

Scientists are talking about different dimensions co-existing; you have seen perhaps programs on TV showing images of dinosaurs crossing your living room, two different worlds unaware of each other, but possibly defying time and space.

Your health

When somebody is asked to define happiness, the first answer is almost always "good health."

If we do not enjoy good health, we may not be able to concentrate and perform to our maximum capacities.

This is why it is so important to take a good look at the state of your health, and at the way you care for it.

You might argue that, going through hard times, you are left with little or no money to go and see a doctor.

In reality, now more than ever you need to be in top physical condition, so you could face hard work and keep an undisturbed mind dealing with a variety of problems. Remember that your family and your future are in your hands; in consequence, if you are well, they will be well.

So keeping your health in good condition is not a luxury, it is a necessity.

And if at all possible, maintain your insurance.

It would not be unusual that during trying times, you feel depressed or experience difficulty sleeping. Again, being in your optimum physical condition is paramount while dealing with stressful situations.

For sleep, try first over-the-counter products, such as Melatonin, Valerian Root or a combination of the two. It is natural and in many instances works quite well; it will give you a restful night, and allow you to start your day with all the energy you need. Advil PM or Tylenol PM could help those with pain conditions.

If you feel depressed, first of all, know that it is a normal feeling in those times and one should expect you to be down when things are not the best in your world; what would be strange is for you to be jumping up and down with joy, while things fall apart around you!

Depression may be a reactional response of a short duration; in this case, you may try St. John's Wort, another over-the-counter natural product.

If your depression is more serious, you must be treated by a professional.

A supplement that I strongly recommend is Omega 3 Fatty Acids found in the old cod liver oil grandma was giving us, and she new what she was doing.

More recently, an extensive Canadian independent medical study, collecting data from some 70 previous studies, came up with scientific proof of the multiple benefits of this product.

It appears that cod liver oil helps a variety of conditions such as arthritis, including rheumatoid arthritis, soft tissue problems like myositis and fibromyalgia, as well as multiple neurological diseases including MS, peripheral neuropathy, and Alzheimer's. All this in addition to the well-known cholesterol lowering benefits.

But it must be the simple, old fashion Omega 3, not others products like Omega 3-6-9, that would cancel the original's product benefits.

If you enjoy a good state of health, (another blessing), make sure you keep it that way.

In any case, observing a healthy life style will be of great benefit for you as well as your family members.

Here are a few simple directions that could be of some help:

Choose the right food

This is a learning process, but there is so much information available, you won't have difficulty choosing foods that you like.

You might like diets such as Mediterranean or South Beach. Very good information you might enjoy, would be reading the book of Doctors Mehmet Oz and Michael Roizen "You Staying Young".

Extremely well documented, accessible to all, you will find good information about the way our body functions, how to prevent diseases, stay healthy and what foods to choose.

You might learn which vitamins or other supplements you need, or what exercises you should introduce in your daily routine.

There are more books written by the same authors, and I would recommend you to consult them; they are very interesting and a lot of fun to read.

Another book I found interesting is "The Blue Zone" by Dan Buettner. Buettner writes about places where people live healthier and longer, and where there are many centenarians.

Buettner describes five "blue zones" in different places in the world with exceptional longevity, having different cultures and eating habits.

Buettner found that in each zone, people maintained an intense physical activity, ate moderately, and cultivated a sense of purpose.

You might find your inspiration in the Mediterranean diet from Sardinia, or from the West Coast of Loma Linda practiced by a community of Seventh Day Adventists.

Personally, although I like to choose carefully the quality of foods, I would not go on a diet; unless you have to follow a diabetic, renal, or hepatic diet, or if you are undernourished and need a hyper caloric diet. I don't see the real need of a getting on a diet.

Time and time again, diets helped people for short periods of times, required stringent restrictions, and failed once they were off the program.

Above all, I don't think anyone could live

constantly on a diet.

What I believe in, though, is to follow a healthy life style. I think that one could find the right balance by combining preferences, cultural flavors, and a variety of nutrients good for the body.

Because of my background, I favor French cuisine; everyone knows that it is not what the standards of diets would describe as "healthy." What I find different in this type of cuisine is that the portions are definitely smaller, although the dishes are quite rich. The ingredients are chosen carefully, always the best quality on the market, and as naturally grown as possible.

This is why, I eat almost everything, and I have kept the same clothing size for the last 30 years; I make a point never to obsess about my weight and I don't have a scale in my bathroom.

Nevertheless, there is no miracle, because my life style includes other elements, I will introduce to you later.

It is common knowledge, that a balanced

"diet" would include lots of fruit and vegetables. I suggest, also, a good amount of proteins and a small quantity of slow carbohydrates. For example, I would have steak and salad, followed by fruit or yogurt as dessert, at dinner or lunch.

I always use olive oil for any uncooked preparation.

Also, I don't use low fat products; in my opinion, I prefer to have a small amount of the best butter, milk, or cheese, and enjoy the taste of "real" food, staying away from processed products.

And I also love chocolate, only dark for me. I make pastry from scratch using old recipes, avoiding quick sweets and trans fats.

Refined sugar and salt are excessively added to already prepared foods, along with saturated fats, and those should be your public enemy number one.

Since this book is not addressing eating problems, I recommend you to refer to the readings mentioned before. However, nowadays, all foods are well labeled, and will give a good indication of their contents, so you can make your choice.

Keep your body hydrated. Water is the best, and it should always be your first choice.
We all are aware of the excessive consumption of sodas and the impact on our health.

It becomes almost another addiction in our modern society.

More recently, some symptoms similar to Multiple Sclerosis have been described in heavy drinkers of diet products containing Glutamate. Fortunately, those symptoms disappeared quickly when users found other alternatives to satisfy their thirst.

When possible, make your own juices. There is no better way of replenishing your body in vitamins and minerals, and having fun with your own, unlimited combinations.

What about alcohol?

This should never be a manner of hydration, must always be used with food, and in moderation. If you enjoy a glass of wine, or a cold beer on a hot day, make it a special occasion only, celebrate special moments, and never drink alcohol habitually.

It upsets the wits out of me when going out to eat, I am just about seated, and here comes the maitre d' (maitre de quelle ceremonie?), stuffing his wine card under my nose. Give me Food! And if I was intending to have a glass of wine, let me see the menu, so I make the right choice of both.

There should always be the best House Tap Water offered first. But again, I can see the economical pressures everywhere.

The same situations are encountered at receptions. Everything starts with liqueur offerings. Liqueur is a beverage offered at the END of dinner. Nothing is more ungraceful than being approached by some tipsy person who doesn't know you, but who already loves you very much!

Sorry for getting so personal!

Exercise

Exercise is great for keeping you in good health, for your mental relaxation while dealing with stress, and even improving your sleep. Often, exercise provides you with the quiet moments you need for getting some clarity in your decisions.

Finding the time and the right disposition might be tough; but everyone knows a few tricks like walking, or taking the stairs when possible, doing a little stretching in the morning and breaking the sedentary habits during the day.

This will also prevent stiffness and pain from setting in, as the day goes on.

Pain could be a serious factor that might make you think you can't exercise. In my profession, I treat patients all day long who are afflicted with conditions accompanied by pain. And I promise you that exercising, with the right timing and type of modalities, is the best way to beat this enemy.

I also assure you that even a few minutes of exercise a day are better than nothing.

If you deal with a chronic or acute, but serious condition, it is best to exercise under professional directions. Slowly and gently, you could progress from total limitation, to as much independence as your body and your will would allow.

I love my medical specialty, Physical Medicine and Rehabilitation and Pain Medicine, because this allows me to care for patients afflicted with all the spectrum of limitations possible. I see many great examples of courage and they are a source of inspiration for all of us. They teach me humility and fill me with admiration everyday.

When I have a bad day and I am ready to start complaining, I think about my patients, and I become ashamed for feeling self-pity, and push myself to go one more mile farther.

I do have a bad back condition though, and many mornings, after a near sleepless night, (I don't take any sedative, since I need to stay clear for potential calls), I feel I can't get out of bed. But I get up, do my exercises religiously seven days a week, and go take care of people in pain.

This is why I believe in exercising, it works!

I could choose to stay in bed and make everybody miserable around me, but I always decide that doing something positive for others is my choice; and guess what, it makes me feel good at the end of the day!

Pain or no pain, I will still have a meaningful and enjoyable life.

Because I know that my days can be unpredictable, and it might not be possible to find the time to exercise later on, I do my routine of stretching, cardio, yoga, etc., in the morning for about 45 minutes. If time permits, I swim laps for 10-15 more minutes, before jumping in the shower and getting ready for work.

I feel energetic and prepared for another good day.

This works for me, but everyone must find the formula that fits their own schedule and preferencces.

A promise

We discussed moments of depression, and that feeling down at times is a normal reaction; we all experience that. What we want to consider here, are those difficult moments when you feel like giving up, overwhelmed by difficulties.

You have the impression that all your efforts are not getting you anywhere, that your prayers are still unanswered, and that you don't see a way out of your problems.

Let me tell you that you are closer than you may think to the arrival of good news; the light at the end of the tunnel is there, you just could not see it yet because you have been so wrapped up in your worries.

It is only a moment in your life and you need to get past that very down moment, to find the rock under your feet, and to give a strong push up. You will hear the song: “there is sunshine after rain."

You will survive this, and come out stronger. And I promise you that later on, when you will look back, you will see the many wonderful reasons you had to stay strong, so you could enjoy many, many more blessings.

Remember what we said about looking for signs, and that sometimes, what we think is best for us, could be a dead end. If you are feeling "stuck" in place, it might be that the wall in front of you stops you from going in the wrong direction, and it is time to turn around and look for a new way out. But who likes to stop and ask for directions?

And above all, remember that ***You Are Not Alone***. Someone down here cares for you, and something a lot greater watches over you from above.

Anticipate the best

A short reminder to start planning ahead, think about potential situations that you can anticipate, and be proactive. Do not be paranoid; don't imagine disasters around every corner, or fear that only bad things can happen.

Remember, what you have in your mind will attract real events.

Now, that you have gotten hold of your situation, it is a lot easier to organize your actions when your mind is clear, and you don't have to act under stress.

It is good to consider what is next, and make the habit of planning your actions. For example, if there is a storm coming, make the necessary preparations, stay calm and under control, and everything will go smoothly. Most of the time there will be no problem, and you won't need to get go into panic mode.

Remember the old saying: "prepare for the worst, and hope for the best."

Anticipation of good and positive things will not only giving you peace of mind, but will save you time and money in the long run.

Your family and you will feel more secure, and this will be a valuable teaching point to your children and others.

Give your blessings

By now, hopefully, your life has already taken a turn for the best; your vision of your place in this world and your future is getting closer to the one of your dreams. I hope that your relationships with your family and friends, and also your encounters with strangers have become more enjoyable.

It may be a good time to start thinking about giving back some of the wisdom, confidence and support you acquired, and share this with others less fortunate than yourself.

Putting your hands on somebody's shoulders, or simply sending them mental messages of light and love will make you feel empowered and elated by those very gestures.

Wish them well, bless them with all your heart, and you, too, will feel the divine energy of your actions.

The love you send out will create a larger trajectory of your Circle of Love, and you will receive more love.

Above all, you will fill the Universe with

goodness and positive energy, and help to purify and reestablish harmony and happiness in our world.

Expand your horizons by travelling

Going places and discovering new ways of living, new cultures could be not only a reward to the sustained efforts you made recently, but a new way of expanding your world as well.

Travels teach us about our beautiful planet, and how similar we are to other people from faraway places, and that human beings all have common problems. When we get to know each other, we find that we are not enemies.

Besides reading books, which is a great way to build character and acquire knowledge, traveling opens our eyes and our hearts to many enriching experiences.

I admired the awesome and exquisite beauty of the Florentine painters, the art of Michelangelo and other great masters, and the layers upon layers of cultural evolution across Europe with its magnificent museums.

Just walking down the streets of these beautiful cities and villages, or admiring the sheer beauty of the Greek islands, will delight you with their multiple ways of expression and creativity of others.

The Far East enchanted me with thousands of years of tradition; and the wonders of the pyramids, the temples on the Nile, from Karnac to Abu Simbel, made me feel so small in front of the mysterious and gigantic work of the ancient Egyptians.

But without doubt, what touched my soul the most were the Holy Places; they were not only magnificent places to visit, but also sites of unique spiritual experiences.

Visiting those blessed grounds, feels like being in front of the gates to Heaven, and will change anyone forever.

It gives the impression that God had chosen these places for holy purposes.

No matter if you are a believer or not, or regardless of your faith, everyone I encountered during my journeys, agreed that there is something special and unexplainable about the Holy sites.

It might sound as a personal testimony, but I feel elated to share a few memories with you.

It is my intention to show that you are not

alone, that I am your friend, and I think that sharing a few souvenirs with you, could give you, too, some of the comfort and certainty that you are protected as well.

My first clear moment that was also a real shock to me, occurred when I was visiting Lourdes, in France. I was very young, and we owned a property close by where we vacationed. It was in winter, a rainy day with nothing like the long lines of pilgrims shown in the movies.

Waiting in a short line to get close to the Grotto of the Pool, where there is also a statue of the Virgin Mary, I was chatting quietly with family, and not trying at all to "psych" myself into any kind of experience.

It was one of the stressful times in my life. In the middle of my sentence, I suddenly felt engulfed by the most loving, peaceful, and celestial feeling one could ever know.

There are no words I could find to describe that incredible sensation; the only one that comes close is Splendor. It was more than an emotion, it was a message that we are not alone; that there is hope beyond belief and that we will be alright.

It goes without saying that my visit to Lourdes changed forever the way I was seeing my life.

Later in life, I had the privilege to see Patmos, a Greek Island, where St. John the Evangelist was exiled by the Roman emperor, had the Revelation and wrote the Book of the Apocalypse.

Walking inside the grotto, touching the rock ceiling split into three parts, one could only feel reverence for the holiness of this place.

Interestingly, seen from above, the shape of the island makes the Alpha and Omega letters, quite a coincidence with the words God addressed to St. John: "I Am the Alpha and the Omega, the Beginning and the End..."

A little farther East in Asia Minor, today part of Turkey, are the ruins of a grandiose Roman city, Ephesus. Close by, is the place where Virgin Mary lived her last years of life. Only a few people know this site; the same for Saint John's Basilica, situated in a village close by, where Saint John's tomb is located.

Entering these places, one tries to imagine living the times of the Scriptures. As it is written in the New Testament, when Jesus entrusted John with Mary's protection, and before He was crucified, He turned to John and said; "here is your mother."

Indeed, in the first half of the first century the Christians started to be persecuted; after St. James was beheaded, John decided it was time to leave Jerusalem, and took Mary to Ephesus. Saint John spread the Christian faith beyond Ephesus, to various cities in Anatolia, and founded the " Seven Churches of Asia Minor." He was already very old, and lived into his late 90's; he is the only Apostle to die from natural causes.

Going to Virgin Mary's house, one has to climb a hill covered with olive trees and beautiful plants and flowers. The beauty of the place is equal only to the peaceful sensation it radiates: again, the overpowering sentiment that ***You Are Not Alone.***

Walking on these blessed grounds, I have never felt more serene and protected. It happened the three times our travels brought us there, and my daughter during our last visit there, was moved to tears.

From that point on, every time I went through difficulties, I imagined being there and feeling again that marvelous loving embrace telling me that I will be OK.

Later on, I learned that the Divine Presence could manifest anywhere; it is only necessary to call upon it. Now, I can sit quietly and meditate, and bring back these unforgettable moments anywhere I am.

In May 2008, my husband and I fulfilled a dream we had for a long time, and visited the Holy Land.

Again the sensation of living the Scriptures, that most of what we were seeing was as it had been in the time of the Scriptures, and that every stone we were walking on, every stone of the homes and streets were still imprinted with 2000 years old images.

Although we read quite a bit over the years about these sites, my personal impression was somewhat different from what I was expecting. It was far more beautiful than I expected, and there is a lot more to see than I imagined.

The places we visited had different atmospheres matching the prominent historical events.

In Jerusalem, we had a clear sensation of oppressive, sad feelings just walking on Via Dolorosa or visiting the Church of Gethsemane with its splendid gardens.

As we progressed North, into Galilee where Jesus lived and began his sermons, I could feel that this is a place where one can easily be in touch with God.

The Sea of Galilee and its surrounding areas, the Mount of Beatitudes, the Jordan River, and Saint Peter's House, are only very few sites to name, each being an experience more enchanting than the other.

It was quite remarkable to notice that some of the areas had the vestiges of multiple cultural constructions: Roman temples, ancient Jewish monuments, along with Christian places, or even Muslim mosques, all blending together.

This could be seen in Jerusalem, where a monolithic entanglement of the three main religions at the Mount Temple, or at the House of Peter surrounded by multiple other monuments of Roman or Jewish origin, gives the impression that God's intention is to have all his children reunited.

Another unexpected surprise was to see how much the Israelis respect and revere Jesus, in particular the younger generation of the Messianic Jews, who, like Christians, are expecting the return of the Messiah.

Learning from other cultures

In some of the preceding chapters, I wrote about valuable lessons one can learn from visiting other countries, and being introduced to different cultures.

A very unique site to visit is the Library of Alexandria. The Library of Alexandria is the oldest, the largest, and the most famous establishment of this nature known in the ancient world.

It originates in the fourth century BC, and was built on the orders of Alexander the Great, who is also the founder of the City of Alexandria which is situated in the northern side of Egypt, on the Mediterranean coast. The area was already under Greek rule.

Alexander the Great died suddenly, at the age of 33, leaving a colossal empire behind.

Nonetheless, his desire was to collect in one place the world's most extensive knowledge.

This was accomplished by Ptolemy I, beginning shortly after Alexander's death. Ptolemy I was the first of a long Greek dynasty in Egypt, stemming from 304 BC to 48 BC, when Julius Caesar defeated Ptolemy XIII.

The members of the Ptolemy dynasty were highly educated, and supporters of arts and sciences. They founded museums and schools, and had their children tutored by the best scholars in Alexandria.

The original building does not exist since a long time; several fires damaged it, with the final destruction attributed to Caliph Omar in 642, when the Arabs conquered Alexandria.

The Library of Alexandria was described by Aristotle to be as an elegant Greek temple.

People were selected from among philosophers, mathematicians, scientists, poets, astronomers, and physicians were mandated to write and share the world's knowledge.

In this place, all information was collected, carefully copied on papyrus scrolls, tagged, and stored. Everything containing the smallest information about other people and their cultures was recorded.

For example, all ships entering the Alexandria

harbor were searched, and if books or any information referring to agriculture, medicine, religion, literature, philosophy, natural sciences, law, history, etc., were found on the ships, those books or information were copied. The copies were returned to the owners, and the originals stored in the Library.

Book collectors searched throughout the world for anything that could enhance the Library's collection.

One can understand that the loss of such an extraordinary wealth of human knowledge left an enormous cultural gap.

In 2002, UNESCO offered the Egyptian nation a new Library of Alexandria, a monument of modern art and technology costing 250 million dollars. Situated close to the site of the old library, Bibliotheca Alexandrina strives to gather as much written information as possible, to fulfill its original purpose.

I visited the Library and the cultural center with its manuscripts, restorations, and archeological museums, library for the blind, and more.

It is impressive and made me feel very hopeful seeing the real desire to preserve precious information for future generations.

Indeed, one can learn that since ancient times in history, early cultures recognized the value of knowledge, the importance of recording information, and the attempts to transmit it to other people.

It is why continuing to pursue our education is so important. It is shown throughout human history, and we should honor the efforts made by men who left us their priceless legacies.

In the same manner, we have the responsibility to help the ones who will follow us to grow as well.

Home sweet home

Like the old adage, "No place like home," everyone who travels the world feels the sweet happiness of coming back home.

It is also the time when one gets to appreciate what a great place we have the good fortune to live in.

Please, include in your blessings list the fact that you wake up every day in this unique country, that you are free and protected.

One should feel wealthy just admiring the beauty and diversity of each region. The cultural and educational resources are practically unlimited and many are quite affordable to visit, and are available to everyone, through our own libraries, institutions, and media.

Most of us enjoy an exceptional quality of life and are our way to fulfilling the American dream, because this country offers the opportunity to so many to accomplish what was once only a hope.

Great achievements, success, and prosperity

are possible for anyone who really puts their mind to it.

Let us not forget the people of this formidable nation, a champion of human rights, and an example of one of the most advanced countries in democracy and technology.

This nation was built by exceptional individuals and many have sacrificed their lives for the good and freedom of others.

Because of their generosity, their high human and moral values, you also have the opportunity to overcome your difficulties, and succeed.

Because you have the chance to live in this place, to be part of this great society, ***You Are Not Alone***.

Conclusion

These last lines are to thank you for reading this book, for getting to the end of it, and hopefully, for learning a few ideas to help you deal with some hard times in your life.

If you have made changes for the better, know that not only did you reach a different and hopefully improved level in your life, but know also that you have taken control of your destiny, and surely you have made yourself and the people around you happier.

If in this book you found some helpful ideas and suggestions, then I am honored, and I sincerely hope that you are closer to where you always dreamed to be.

From now on, please look up, smile, and go live the happiest life possible!

Acknowledgements

This book was written at the insistence of my patients. Over the years they have asked me to put in writing some of the encouragements or advices I was giving them. During consultations, I often made simple comments or suggestions, and then as we progressed, we searched together for ways of solving problems.

In no way did I intend to make this a complicated, psychological dissertation, but a rather down-to-earth, simple reading coming from the heart.

Thanks to these special moments I shared with my patients, the good that sometimes resulted in their lives, and also the lessons I learn from their courage, I found the inspiration to write this book with the hope that it will help others to uplift their spirits.

My heartfelt thanks go naturally to these very special people, my patients.

Growing up I was like a sponge striving to absorb what others have shown in their teachings or accomplishments.

Any of my achievements were definitely influenced by learning from other cultures or people's experiences, and my readings.

Sometimes I could remember some author's work and many times it was stored in my memory, when situations or feelings would cause those deep impressions made by a work of art, writing, or event to resurface.

Whenever it was possible, I tried to name and recognize the sources of my inspiration, and the great value I attribute to these works; I also want to share those learning experiences with my reader.

I am sure that without any ill intention, some of the images or situations came naturally from my readings. It has never been my intention to appropriate the authenticity of these writings.

Any names, situations, or descriptions contained in this book are the product of my own interpretation.

In some occasions I provided citations from universal readings such as the Bible, quotations that are available to all, and my intention was to open the door to my readers to go further into those readings.

My thanks go to my family and friends. I feel very blessed for their presence, and the great influence they had in my life.

I feel very fortunate to have Beatrice, my daughter, whose beauty, sense of humor and talents graced my life even at the most difficult passages. She is the reason that, many times, kept me going. And presently, she brings me great happiness with her little family.

My final thoughts will always go to Robert, my husband and my best friend, for always being there for me, for the laughter, the encouragements, and his wisdom, and for the ultimate and best journey we share together, our marriage.

Reader reviews

Growth and Self-Knowledge - This book is written in a friendly, easy to read manner. I cannot imagine anyone who would not benefit from this book. Dr. Monk takes you on a ride that helps your understanding of yourself. Your confidence booms, and your problems all seem manageable with the knowledge she shares with the reader.

Read it. You will not be sorry!

N. McKenzie, resident, northwest Florida

Looking at the Silver Linings - All of us face tragedy and sometimes feel that we won't recover, but Dr. Monk encourages the reader to look beyond the loss of the past to the opportunities in the future. The universe does support us, but it doesn't do that by allowing us to stay stuck in the past--it forces change, even when we feel we aren't ready for it.

Ron Frazer, PhD, author of "The Judge's Wife", "The Carib's Smile", "A Handful of Seawater", "Sandscript", "The Blackwater

Review", and "The African-American Review"

Words of Inspiration - Dr. Monk takes the reader through many of life's ups and downs, and talks about surviving the downs and cherishing the ups. Nothing worthwhile is easy, but you can achieve your dreams if you believe in yourself. In the short time I have the book, I have picked it up to reread when I had a situation I thought unbearable. Her words helped me find my direction and get back on track. This is a lovely, feel good, short book that I am sure will be inspiration to all readers looking for inspiration.

B. Leigh, frequent Amazon reviewer

17540086R00070

Made in the USA
Charleston, SC
16 February 2013